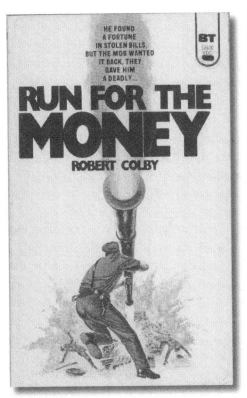

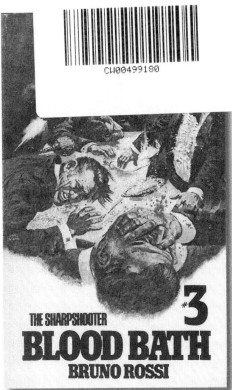

THE SHARPSHOOTER

BLOOD BATH

BRUNO ROSSI

#3

CW00499180

Lo-fi, lo-budget and lo-IQ, but never lo-energy, this is Men of Violence.

In 2016 the ultimate artist in the men's adventure genre passed away. Ken Barr's paintings for series such as The Marksman, The Sharpshooter and The Hunter were the very embodiment of all that I love about this much maligned genre. Exciting, bombastic and teetering on the ludicrous, Barr's dynamic figures and compositions exploded from the page.

I can't add any flesh to Barr's biography over and above on-line sources (including a bio from an old Warren monster mag) and the art book *The Beast Within*. Needless to say, his work has always left his mark on me, from his photo-realistic renderings of Marvel characters such as The Hulk through to his cover paintings for cheap-jack paperbacks from Belmont Tower, Leisure, Manor and Fawcett Crest.

Has there EVER been a better men's adventure cover than *Blood Bath*? You can't even begin to imagine how many cruddy books were sold because of a Ken Barr cover. This issue is dedicated to the memory of Ken Barr.

BRONSON!

The commercial success of the vigilante hero for lower-rung paperback publishers in the 1970's, generated little in the way of obvious film equivalents.

Super-sleazy and gritty exploitationer, *The Exterminator* (1980) is undoubtedly the truest to its pulp cousins, with one cop 'accidentally' calling the titular vigilante "The Executioner", and Sylvester Stallone is reputed to be a pulp fan, with the ludicrous *Cobra* (1986) his paean to the genre.

But I would imagine that the example that springs to most people's mind is *Death Wish*, Michael Winner's crude-yet-powerful 1974 film which was a commercial success. It meant lead actor Charles Bronson became a model for certain paperback artists, or even a character name in the case of the you-gotta-love-them Manor Books. I suspect that not as many of you will be familiar with Brian Garfield's source novel of 1972, and it too had sat unread on the shelves until recent curiosity got the better of me and I read both it, and sequel *Death Sentence* (1975) over a few days.

  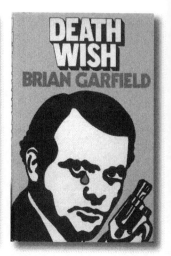

Men of Violence 5 and 6 reprint

Compared to the intense and rugged film adaptation, *Death Wish* the book is far slower and less action-packed (two thirds of the pages have unfolded until Paul Benjamin's first act of violence), more interested in building a picture of how a liberal accountant can be transformed into a vigilante who quite frankly is psychotic. It certainly is far less lurid than the film, with the fate of Benjamin's wife and daughter kept off-screen (Winner would receive a lot of criticism about his depiction of their ordeal in this and the follow-up films) and the set-pieces much smaller and over in the blink-of-an-eye.

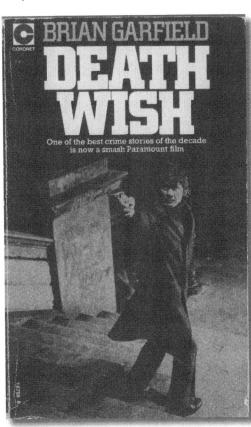

BRIAN GARFIELD

DEATH WISH

One of the best crime stories of the decade is now a smash Paramount film

The book's tone is neutral, with several narrative voices expressing apposite political viewpoints, whilst Garfield focuses on Paul Benjamin's mental disintegration. This is very different to the film adaptation which on the surface is far more right-wing with its old school testament philosophy. Judging by the film's commercial success (especially compared to the book, to which the rights were only sold as part of a multi-book package) and urban legends of audience members in cinemas shouting encouragement to Benjamin's character, British director Winner undoubtedly tapped into the zeitgeist of America.

The original vision for the film may well have been very different to Winner's finished product. Apparently the film was originally slotted to be directed by Sidney Lumet with Jack Lemmon in the lead, but the producers went broke and sold the rights to *Death Wish* and *Serpico* (Garfield had been one of the "super-cop's" first ghost-writers). Garfield's public criticism of Winner's vision was considered by the author to be a major factor in Winner and Bronson later withdrawing from a Donald Westlake adaptation that Garfield had screen-played.

Garfield's dissatisfaction with Winner's execution of his material was undoubtedly a motivator in

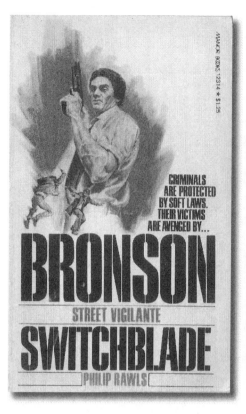

him penning follow-up, *Death Sentence*, in which Benjamin has relocated to Chicago and continues his vigilante mission. The book opens where the previous one ends, with Benjamin searching for criminals to punish. Staggering around the ghettos pretending to be drunk, he initially fails to attract any attention (a playful inversion of the normal conventions where such locales are solely populated with predatory criminals), but soon begins to entrap and then shoot people for the smallest infractions (darkly satirical British comics character Judge Dredd was created a few years after this book, and extrapolated Benjamin to a ludicrous extreme).

Very much a riposte to the simple-minded eye-for-an-eye fantasy of the film, *Death Sentence* is written in a much more detached style than its predecessor and fills in the space from the first novel that allowed the reader to apply their own interpretation of Benjamin's actions. Its tone is nearer to journalistic, with Garfield featuring crime reporters as key characters and presenting Benjamin's exploits as newspaper reports, further removing that vicarious thrill of reading the acts of retribution presented in the dramatic language of fiction.

Garfield's follow-up is much more concerned with the ripple affect of Benjamin's actions on wider society. There is not the simple "retribution equals redemption" message of the film, as Benjamin accidentally kills a teenager during one of his missions, triggers off several copy-cat vigilantes and creates a shoot-first, question-later culture amongst both criminals and their victims.

Again, Garfield's source novel did not receive an especially faithful adaptation for its 2007 film version, but in interviews I've seen, seemed happier that this was a by-product of the decades aging the original book and the 2007 film addressing more of the philosophical themes of his work than the Winner adaptation. I read on-line that a remake of *Death Wish*, starring Bruce Willis who strikes me as perfect for the role of Benjamin, is underway.

I found Garfield to be a thoughtful and skilful author who shows a great control of his craft and delivered a very different product to one that I had expected after the film versions. Both books are interesting curio items due to their wider influence on popular culture and as an example of a more mainstream and rooted version of the men's adventure novel. Despite their significance in moving men's adventure into mainstream best-sellerdom, I do not think either novel is particularly worthy of revisiting. There are other titles in Garfield's solid catalogue which I would rather point you in the direction of.

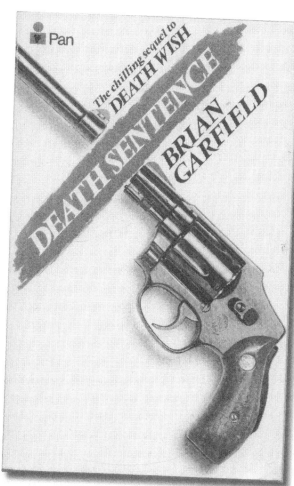

THE LAST COWBOY

Brian Garfield, best known as author of *Death Wish*, has produced a consistently interesting body of work in the thriller genre, typically looking to the traditions of the western novel for his stories of revenge, lone-wolf heroes and impossible odds.

He is noteworthy for his inventive plots which bought him to the attention of the film industry, with his script (co-written with Donald Westlake) for the 1987 cult horror flick *The Step Father* a stand-out.

Garfield was born in 1939, in New York, where he would later set his most famous novel, but grew up in Arizona, so it was inevitable he would work in the western genre. Aged 16, he approached western author Luke Short (real name Fred Glidden) who lived locally and who was happy to share his wisdom.

Men of Violence 5 and 6 reprint

Only two years later, 18-year old Garfield produced his first western; *Range Justice* was published by Avalon Books, who specialised in providing books for libraries. It did not see print for three years, by which time he was serving in the Army.

Across the 1960's Garfield produced in the region of 25 western paperbacks, most notably for Ace Books where he used the pseudonyms Frank Wynne and Brian Wynne and produced eight books in a 'Justin Six' series. He also provided *Buchanan's Gun* (1968) as Jonas Ward in the **Buchanan** series for Fawcett, where he joined the likes of Robert Silverberg in stepping into the boots of

the deceased William Ard who was the original Ward.

Garfield had formed a friend-ship with Westlake and fellow crime author Laurence Block and enjoyed regular poker sessions with them in the mid-60s. Although I have absolutely zero evidence to back it up, I wonder if Garfield contributed to any of the sleaze paperback houses where Westlake and Block in particular were so productive in the 1960s. Westlake and Garfield collaborated, most notably on *Gangway!* (1973) a comedy western novel and later, on the screenplay for *The Stepfather*. Garfield also produced a screenplay of Westlake's Stark novel *Butcher's Moon* (1974) that was never made, possibly due to

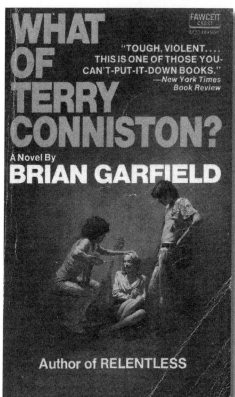

heist thrillers with a comedic twist.

Garfield tended not to use recurring characters unless the publisher demanded it, but Arizona cop Sam Watchman had two novels; *Relentless* (1972) and *The Threepersons Hunt* (1975). Both are superior thrillers, with the former title working on several levels; describing the five bank robbers on the run, Watchman's drive to track them down, and the blizzard conditions that swallow up the chase. Apparently it was made into a TV movie in 1977. Watchman was loosely based on a Navajo classmate of Garfield's from University who also provided a number of anecdotes which Gar-

Garfield's criticism of Michael Winner's adaptation of *Death Wish*.

In the 1970's there was a noticeable shift of direction into thrillers under his own name, as if Garfield had decided that he paid his dues as a jobbing pulp writer in the previous decade and was now ready to further evolve. *What of Terry Conniston?* (1971) was an inventive thriller of the kidnapping gone wrong of the titular rock star, which showed the influence of Westlake who wrote the Parker series as Richard Stark and produced a steady stream of

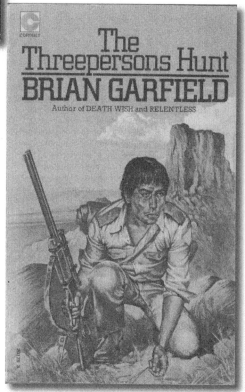

field used as material for the books.

Later that decade Garfield began to use pseudonyms again; *Target: Manhattan* (1975) by Drew Mallory has a cracker-jack idea but unfortunately the book doesn't quite deliver on this potential. The titular city is held to ransom by a team of aviation buffs who are circling in a world war two bomber threatening to drop its pay-load of bombs. Garfield's pair of revenge-thrillers as John Ives are better, especially *Fear in a Handful of Dust* (1978), the account of five doctors who are cast adrift in the burning Arizona desert without any clothes, food or water as part of a revenge plot by a Vietnam veteran they sectioned for war crimes. With an insistence on documenting and using actual survival

techniques, it brings to mind David Morrell's *Testament* (1975) also reviewed in this issue. It was adapted into a low-budget film as *Flesh Burn* (1984) which is available on You Tube.

CORONET

Relentless
BRIAN GARFIELD

A gripping tale of flight and pursuit from a highly talented storyteller

THE MARCHAND WOMAN

A
ONE
WOMAN
ARMY
A NOVEL BY
JOHN IVES

That Marchand Woman (1979) was a lesser book, but still tightly-plotted and nimble-footed, the account of a mother seeking justice for her son's death at the hands of revolutionaries. Set on a much larger international scale than Garfield's model *Death Wish* and with little of the intellect or desire to provoke debate. I preferred it.

In many ways Brian Garfield is that most peculiar of creatures, the intellectual liberal who

produced men's adventure novels. For the most part, he was never able to fully ditch the liberal politics and they typically weighed down his books.

Interestingly enough, when he put the preaching to one side, in the case of *Death Wish*, the interpretation of his audience horrified him. He never really left the western genre, using desert settings and one man against impossible odds, or the sheriff-figure bringing justice to a frontier town, many many times.

FINGER ON THE TRIGGER

Throughout the 1970's, the early parts in particular, survivalism was a recurrent theme in popular culture. In films people were under siege from zombies in *Night of the Living Dead*, slaughter-house workers in *Texas Chainsaw Massacre*, mutant in-breds in *The Hills Have Eyes*, gang-members in *Assault on Precinct 13* and by native Creoles in *Southern Comfort*.

In paperbacks you had *Straw Dogs* and *Deliverance*, both of which are more famous for their celluloid adaptations, and the title I want to discuss, *Testament* (1975) by David Morrell.

Morrell is now best known as author of *First Blood* (1972), an excellent book which was turned into a decent film, and for his ability to genre-hop, with horror (*The Totem, Creepers*) and crime (*League of Night and Fog*) titles also under his belt. There is no doubting that Morrell is a master crafts person and when not producing successful books, has taught English literature as well as writing 'How Tos' for aspiring authors.

Testament was Morrell's second published work, and like *First Blood*, shares themes of violence and of a man confronted with difficult choices. In the case of Reuben Bourne, a freelance writer with a young family, he is not built to handle the physical elements of confrontation a la John Rambo, but is forced to when he makes the mistake of running an expose on Kess, a militia leader.

TESTAMENT

'TERRORS AS INSISTENT AS A SCREAM ON A STILL NIGHT, AS A SERIES OF KICKS IN THE STOMACH...BRILLIANTLY TOLD' SUNDAY TELEGRAPH

FROM THE AUTHOR OF FIRST BLOOD
DAVID MORRELL

Men of Violence 5 and 6 reprint

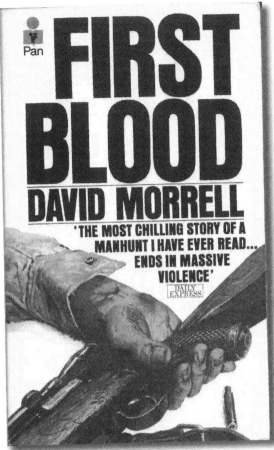

With an underground army at his disposal, Kess, the home-grown terrorist/freedom fighter (delete based on your political views) begins a campaign of retribution, with Bourne's children in his trigger-sights as much as the reporter.

My 1977 paperback edition from Pan UK, is plastered with strident reviews which mark the book out as a classic of its kind. I think it very much is a book of its time, written with absolute sincerity, title thundering with biblical significance, asking the *big* questions about violence in a society fresh off the TV coverage of Vietnam.

It's a brutal read. Morrell totally bludgeons the reader with one shock after the other. And they are truly shocking - one scene involving Bourne's daughter had me saying "No, no, no" out loud. By the end I was as weary as Bourne and his family following their escape route through an inhospitable mountains landscape

Its climax is controversial and very much at odds to the conventional behaviour of the male lead in this type of novel. To such an extent I imagine Morrell's publishers would have attempted to change it.

It could have been even more revelatory if Morrell had not pushed the reader so hard in the previous 200 pages. By this stage, I

was so punch-drunk, I welcomed the final knock-out blow.

Morrell had undoubtedly undertaken his research, which included mountain survival training to understand the challenges that Bourne and family undertake. I've never been a stickler for technical detail, so these elements of the book were initially interesting but soon began to wear on me. On the opposite end of the scale was the manner in which Kess' men popped up no matter how remote the location as well as their infiltration of all elements of government. This paranoia turned up to 11 distracted me from the realistic vibe Morrell was striving so hard to achieve.

In his essay in *Thrillers 100 Must Reads*, Morrell praises Geoffrey Household's *Rogue Male* (1939) as an outstanding example of the genre and a major influence on his writing. It was the full-blooded and visceral approach of Household, specially *Rogue Male*'s blistering four-page opening sequence, that helped develop his writing style. I can definitely see this reflected in *Testament*'s short, punchy chapters, especially chapter one which is only three pages, but three pages I guarantee you will not forget quickly.

It starts with, "It was the last morning the four of them would ever be together: the man and his wife, his daughter and his son."

I suggest you strap yourself in and start from there.

TRIPLE-BLADED

One of the more idiosyncratic and downright bizarre aspects of behaviour from the paperback fanatic is the collection of a certain cover motif. This can take many forms, and one motif that I collect are paperbacks with weaponry as a key image. I own paperbacks, most of which I will never read, with cover images of broken bottles, spanners, knuckle-dusters, bike-chains, machetes, bed-springs, harpoons and my personal favourite, the straight razor. (As we all obviously know, covers with whips are a whole 'nother sub-genre)

Easy to conceal, carried to disfigure rather than kill, and used up close and personal, there is something quintessentially nasty about a razor. Social history is full of legends of razor gangs ready to carve up anyone that got in their way, so it's little wonder that paperback authors and publishers used the weapon to add that element of frisson to their wares. Possibly the most famous is Josiah Hedges, the western anti-hero who wielded a straight-edge and even took his nickname Edge from one, setting a template for many future "adult western" leads to be named after phallic weapons.

Pan Books led with razor imagery on at least three paperbacks that I know of, with two being of potential interest to readers of **Men of Violence**.

Two major social trends reflected in paperback originals of the 1970's were the influence of *Death Wish* (covered elsewhere in this issue – it's as if I plan this stuff!) and the growth of women's liberation. Not every man was keen on the emancipation of women, and this was often reflected in men's adventure fiction, with a growing number of sex-crazed, double-crossing Mafioso mistresses popping up in series such

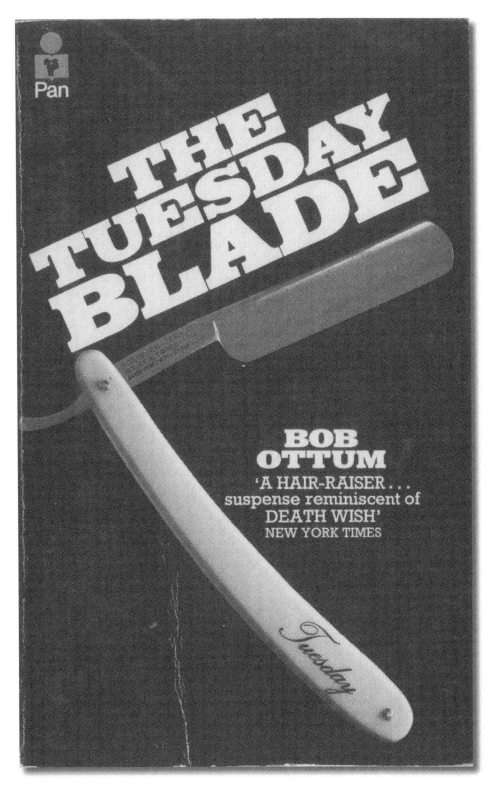

THE TUESDAY BLADE

Pan

BOB OTTUM

'A HAIR-RAISER . . .
suspense reminiscent of
DEATH WISH'
NEW YORK TIMES

Tuesday

Men of Violence 5 and 6 reprint

as **The Marksman** and **The Sharpshooter**. Valerie Solanos and her SCUM (Society for Cutting Up Men) Manifesto had redblooded hacks typing with one-hand while they protectfully cradled their nut-sacks with the other!

Bob Ottum's debut novel, *The Tuesday Blade* (1977) is, in my view, a reflection of both of these trends. And I suspect, a reflection of some of Ottum's own views, although I have no evidence to back this up. It follows the man-hating vendetta of Glory-Ann, who using the personalised straight-razor of a pimp that had abused her, proceeds to gut and

castrate several horny New Yorkers, earning her the nickname "Jill the Ripper" (what a great title for a book!). Ottum doesn't hold back on the razor attacks which are ripe with loops of guts and dissected scrotums.

I was looking forward to this read as I plan a future special issue called **Women of Violence**, but this was as sleazy, misogynistic and un-sympathetic to women as any example of the men's adventure genre. At no point do you feel any sympathy with Glory-Ann's actions, and she just falls into the giant morass of unlikable characters that populate *The Tuesday Blade*.

Ottum outlines Glory-Ann's formative teenage years with rather too much relish for my personal comfort; a gang rape that verges on the fetishistic in its portrayal, and plentiful passages on the development of her bulging biceps. It's creepy stuff, and you can visualise the beads of sweat popping out on the writer's forehead as he typed these scenes out.

Of some interest because of the attitudes it undoubtedly reflected and the unrestrained execution by Ottum.

Before diversifying into children's books (the mind boggles...), Ottum followed this shocker up with *See The Kid Run* (1978) which traced the career of a J.D. punk with similarly nauseating results (which I know some of you will take as the highest recommendation!).

Run Down (1970) by Robert Garrett, welcomed readers to "The violent world of Alan Brett – a man who cannot be stopped", beating the Berkley Medallion in US to the punch(line) by several years, when they repackaged Donald Westlake's books as "The violent world of Parker".

Brett has the standard back story of murdered-wife-turns-him-into-one man-killing machine, now accepting contracts from the shadier arms of British government to wipe-out The Syndicate who are major movers in international heroin trade. Brett starts at the bottom of the food-chain, and soon his success in eradicating each successive layer of management in The Syndicate turns into an extended job-interview to join that criminal organisation. At the climax he comes face to face with The Ostrich, who offers Brett the chance to be reunited with his wife (who may not have been murdered after all), in return for a "favour" which will bring down the British secret service.

Primarily set around a seedy Soho, this is super-cynical, hob-nailed-boots-tough story-telling, evidently influenced as much by Ted Lewis of *Get Carter* fame as the likes of Ian Fleming. Brett is amoral, dour and calculat-

ing, perfectly suited to his task and scatter-gunning sardonic one-liners to his boss and the reader. At one point he has no compunction in torturing a member of The Syndicate with a red-hot poker (now that would be a cover image!) with Garrett laying it on strong with the sizzling flesh and uttered profanities. There are several excellent scenes in which Brett is faced with impossible odds, yet takes a practical and straight-forward approach. In particular, the manner in which he gains entrance to a Soho night-club was very reminis-

A terrifying new novel from the author of
THE TUESDAY BLADE

See the Kid Run

BOB OTTUM

cent of the scene where Carter interrupts a card game in the film version.

Unfortunately the cover image of a brutal hand-to-hand fight in a cramped toilet doesn't portray a scene from the book, although at one point Brett does tape a straight-razor to his leg as a back-up weapon. I like the dressings in the photo which give that truly seedy feel – a copy of **Playboy** and cleaning products on the window-sill.

In the author bio, it states that *Run Down* was Garrett's first book, and that he had quit employment at Midland Bank (shades of pulp horror legend Guy N Smith) to take several part-time jobs while he focused on his writing. It doesn't appear that he was successful, as beyond *Spiral* (1972) a follow-up, there are no other books I can trace under his name. I can only speculate that Brett was too hard-boiled and unrelenting for the British reading public.

Run-Down is a very apt title and a real treat if you like your men's adventure fiction full-throttled and brutal. And I've only just clocked that if you shorten the authors name to Bob, you can see how he named his character. B(ob Ga)rett!

For the sake of completeness I've also run the cover image from *The Power House* (1968) by William Haggard, which part of his Colonel Charles Russel series. Haggard was a pseudonym for Richard Clayton, who as a civil servant was very much part of the British establishment and this book reflects that. It's a thriller focused on a MP defecting to communist Russia with a sub-plot about underworld gambling but overly focused on class and politics, with little to recommend to readers of **Men of Violence**.

Pan Books

ROBERT GARRETT

RUN DOWN

The violent world of Alan Brett – a
man who cannot be stopped

Men of Violence 5 and 6 reprint

PAN SPIES OF THE 60's

One of the more interesting and shady tactics of publishers, is to see off imitations of their successful characters and titles from rival publishers by flooding the market with their own imitations. Pinnacle were a noticeable practitioner of such tactics, launching The Penetrator, The Death Merchant and The Butcher on the back of The Executioner's success, with at least one of those in response to the very real possibility that a rival publisher was going to hijack The Executioner. A decade earlier, Pan Books, who in the UK had enjoyed huge sales with paperback editions of James Bond, ran at least three series in a direct response to reader demand, all with James Bond-esque names— Dr. Jason Love, Charles Hood and Hugo Baron.

Dr. Jason Love

Of the three series, James Leasor's accounts of country Doctor and car enthusiast turned part-time spy was undoubtedly the most commercially successful. There were nine burning hunks of Love, with six repackaged for paperback by Pan Books. Early titles were distinguished by using the word "Passport" in the title, although after four they switched to "Love". A move which I imagine was designed to make it clear to audiences that it was a Jason Love adventure, but always struck me as misjudged and better suited to a light-hearted romance series.

Love's first adventure, *Passport to Oblivion* (1964) was a big-seller in the 1960's, going through a couple of printings per year, including a film tie-in edition in 1965 when Val Guest directed his vision of the Bond-rival. Guest's career went into free-fall in the 1970's, a sad end to the man behind two genre-defining Quatermass films. David Niven was his Jason Love, an incongruous choice by today's standards of

PAN books X552

DIECAST
John Michael Brett

HUGO BARON
Man-about-danger
'How like Bond and
just as good'
DAILY EXPRESS

Men of Violence 5 and 6 reprint

masculinity, an actor that stayed in the spy game for the disastrous spoof *Casino Royale* (1967) and *Assignment K* (1968).

Leasor followed what is now a well-recognised path in British fiction-writers; well-educated in London and Oxford, he served in the Army in Burma during the Second World War, then joined the Daily Express newspaper as a columnist and foreign correspondent. In the mid-50's he resigned to pursue his career in books, initially building on his journalistic strengths by producing historical and war-time non-fiction. When *Passport* was a hit, he focused on Love's adventures for a decade.

Already wielding a naturally dry writing style that resembled Fleming's, rumour has it that Leasor was once approached to pen a Bond sequel, an opportunity he declined. As the spy-boom faded and presumably Leasor became financially secure, he switched from Love back to non-fiction. Again, he was commercially successful, most notably when his account of a previously undocumented World War Two Mission was filmed as *The Sea Wolves* (1980).

Jason Love is a doctor practicing out of rural South West England, but doesn't fit the stereotype; burning up the country lanes in his Cord roadster, teaching local judo classes and enjoying the finest wines and ladies known to humanity. In the opening book, *Passport to Oblivion*, an experi-

enced agent goes missing in Tehran (this sequence, adroitly written in a knowing tone is fantastic, but unfortunately the rest of the book fails to match), the Secret Service sees a doctor's convention as the prefect cover to slip in an agent. Lacking a credible employee, they conscript Love who is piqued by the challenge of being a part-time spy. Once in Tehran, Love is drawn ever deeper into a labyrinth assassination plot.

Based on their longevity and a film, I was expecting much more from the Love novels. *Passport to Oblivion* has all of bells and whistles you might require of a Bond style international intrigue adventure, and was understandably successful amongst a reading public eager for more Fleming-style thrills. There are occasional flashes of excellence such as the opening sequence which I felt promised so much, or when Love is cornered in a hotel room by two assassins who are too professional to fall for his desperate tricks. But those are notable because of their irregularity, and ultimately this is a book I did not mind putting down at night, and did not feel any anticipation when opening it again the next day. I tried *Love All* (1971), with similar results ("Fuck all!" you might say), but wonder if *A Week in Love* (1960), which was seven short stories, might offer a more rewarding read due to the difference in structure in the short-form.

Men of Violence 5 and 6 reprint

Charles Hood

James Mayo, the credited author of the six Charles Hood books has as much of an air of mystery about him as his fictional super-spy. Although most on-line sources list Mayo as a pseudonym of Stephen Coulter, little can be found out about Coulter which has led to speculation that BOTH Mayo and Coulter are pseudonyms. Apparently the man behind Mayo name had begun his career in journalism, before serving in Navy intelligence for Eisenhower, especially in post-war France. The latter furnished him with the background detail to help his colleague, a certain Ian Fleming, with research to the gambling scene in *Casino Royale*, persuading Fleming not to drop what is now regarded as a classic sequence. And I guess, also persuading Mayo/Coulter to turn their pen to fiction.

Like Dr. Jason Love, Charles Hood is a part-time spy, his career as a world-class sportsman over and his living now made as a successful art-dealer. Extra-curricular thrills are provided by the Circle, a shadowy intelligent agency made up of philanthropists who wish to keep world peace, and occasionally employ Hood to those ends. There were six Hood adventures in paperback at Pan from 1964 to 1971, with *Hammerhead* (1964), the first story, probably the best known as it was adapted into a film in 1968. In the novel, titular Hammerhead is a sadistic villain with two mistresses and a huge porn- ahem – erotica collection, who has stolen a top-secret weapon to destroy the world.

Unlike Leasor, who as mentioned, mimicked Fleming's dry narrative style, Coulter evidently made a decision to out-Bond Bond on every level, with even more fast-switching international locations, even more outlandish villains and even more doe-eyed love interests. In *Hammerhead*, Hood is buried alive in a coffin, in *Let Sleeping Girls Lie* (1965), Hood is staked out as the hors d'oeuvres for a vulture trained to eat live human flesh, and in *The Man Above Suspicion* (1969), a thug wielding a giant bull-whip plays cat-and- mouse with a motor-biking Hood in a deserted zoo! With a straight-forward pared-down style, and all the dubious sexual politics of that era, It's Bond with the volume turned up to 11 and it held much more appeal to my pulpy tastes than Dr. Love.

There was also a Hood film, with an adaptation of the first book made in 1968 by a British producer and starring Diana Dors, Judy Geeson and Vince Edwards. Based on snippets I've watch online, once you get past the ludicrous opening sequence, it's a faithful adaptation.

Hugo Baron

There were three entries to the Hugo Baron series, and I wish there had been more as I found it to be the most intriguing and twisted of the trio. Baron is a barrister (lawyer to our American cousins) who is foot-loose and impulsive, and finds a straight-forward piece of freelance advice work for Paul Lorenz, a press millionaire who is being blackmailed, turns into something sinister. And here is where it gets interesting for me – spoiler ahead– as the megalomaniacal press bar-

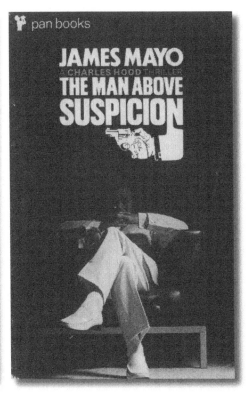

Men of Violence 5 and 6 reprint

on has bank-rolled D.I.E.C.A.S.T. a peace-through-violence organisation, and wants to recruit the quite frankly, psychotic, Baron as his latest agent.

It's a standard foe in the form of the Communists, but it's the use of Baron as a very flawed hero and the monstrous Lorenz as his bankroller that sets this series apart with its very dark tone. At one point Lorenz shows Baron footage of the torture of an agent who decided to leave D.I.E.C.A.S.T. which seems to have little impact on either man. Are these supposed to be the good guys? I am not sure if author John Michael Brett (actually Miles Tripp) intended Baron to be an anti-hero, or that in the 60's, Baron and in particular Lorenz, could be seen as heroic. A frightening thought indeed, especially in Britain where the likes of Rob-

ert Maxwell and the tabloid press have a disgraceful history.

In *A Plague of Dragons* (1966), Baron's adventure take an exotic turn with a chase across Egypt and Kenya, as he attempts to unveil the fiendish plot of Dr. Kwang, a Fu Manchu for the 1960. The same year saw the release of *A Cargo of Spent Evil*, but I do not own a copy. The packaging of the books is the closest of the three series to that of Bond, with effective montages by an unknown artist in the style of a film poster. From a distance, it would be say for the casual book browser to presume the arm-folded and gun-wielding figure was Bond. Baron also had his own logo, complete with dice.

As mentioned, Miles Tripp used the pseudonym of Brett for the trilogy, and like Leasor and Mayo employs a clipped and economic prose style. Tripp keeps the action more steeped in realism than the others, and Baron is often desperate in his actions, rather than conventionally heroic. Take one scene where he is cornered by the heavies and to avoid a sound thrashing, shins up a lamp-post and stamps on the fingers of anyone attempting to clamber up after him. He completes his escape by diving through the window of a squalid flat on the same level as the lamp-post, and attracting the attention of the passing police. It's gritty, dirty, street-level action.

Apparently Tripp had trained as a solicitor, so maybe it was inevitable that he would feature someone in the legal trade as his first hero. He went onto create a Private Detective character, John Samson, and would spend most of his later writing career documenting his adventures. I have not read any Tripp, but own a couple of Pans under his own name, of which *The Fifth Point of the Compass* (1967) looks most interesting. Based on the back cover blurb, an eleven-year old boy is set a survival test by his father, the arrogant owner of a Canadian air-line.

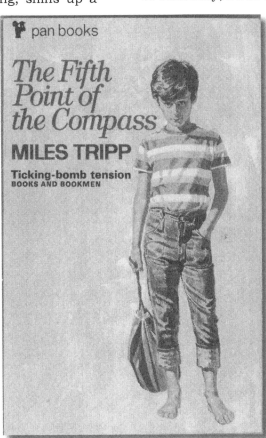

In summary, I was disappointed by the three series I explored for this article, despite the perverse glee I extracted from Hugo Baron's twisted take on heroics. Compared to the men's adventure novels of the 1970's, they were very dated in their politics, outlook and style, and were too close to Bond in their execution. Charles Hood was the closest to really letting loose, showing some real gusto at times, but did not do it often enough to take the books to the next level.

I think the French were the masters of the Bond-rip-off, with characters such as Malko and Agent OSS-117, which I plan to cover in a future issue.

BEST OF THE TOUGH COPS

Award Books never seemed to make much of a concerted effort in the men's adventure market, focusing all their resource into their successful Nick Carter franchise, but The Liquidator series is the best of the rest. Although there are a few snippy reviews posted on-line of The Liquidator series, I would consider the first book (I have not read the others) to be a superior example of the tough-cop/lone-wolf genre.

Lead character Jake Brand becomes a police-man when his all-American brother (a college quarter-back who gave it up to serve in the Korean war) is blasted by the Mafia, showing scant regard for his own life as he uses his badge and gun as the tools in his one-man vendetta, which earns him constant ass-chewings from his weary commander. Eventually the Mafia decides to do away with Brand, utilising a more ingenious method than normally demonstrated in this type of book. Of course, it doesn't work, so Brand returns to continue his mission, this time, totally outside the law.

Award Books have a reputation for being very Southern-based in their approach to content and distribution, which means they rarely deviate into material that is too salacious or outrageous (they also published Beacon and Softcover Library lines, which as "sleaze" were very different animals), and The Liquidator is cut from the same cloth. However, where it rises beyond the mediocre is in the deceptively simple yet involving story-line and the hard-boiled atmospherics.

With his ludicrous machismo, brick-jaw and buzz cut, Brand is an early prototype for a character in the Frank Miller **Sin City** comic books. A juggernaut in human form, he busts down doors with his shoulders and knees hoods in the balls as if it were a Olympic sport. Brand operates in a world of smoky pool-halls and semi-legit dance clubs worked by hookers with hearts of gold, while his love interest is all soft curves, blonde curls and ruby-red lips.

Although the copyright records show The Liquidator series as 'work for hire' for Award, perceived wisdom is that Larry Powell wrote them. I know very little about Powell, but a few on-line searches threw up some snippets. As well as The Liquidator books, Powell also produced a couple of Nick Carters for Award in 1973, specifically *The Code* and The Butcher of Belgrade. It is possible that Powell produced other Award books, or even sleazers for the aforementioned Softcover/Beacons. Nearly a decade later, he is credited for the third book in the Able Team series, *Texas Showdown* (1982). I have not read it, but imagine that Powell's style may have been dated by the early eighties and not suited to the genre requirements of the time, which is possibly why I see no others.

THE LIQUIDATOR
THE EXCHANGE
R. L. BRENT

CHARTER/72210-2 $1.75

The Mob's Porno King has a high-level hostage—and Jake Brand has sworn revenge!

Previous to his Award Books, I can find some ink traces of Powell in digest and sweat mags of the 1960. The earliest being 'The Spider and the Fly' which appeared in the September 1965 edition of **Man's Magazine**, which was published by Pyramid who as I am sure you will know, also had a paperback line. The following year, he had 'Partner in Crime' in a 1966 edition of **Men's Digest**, one of the digest mags from Cam-

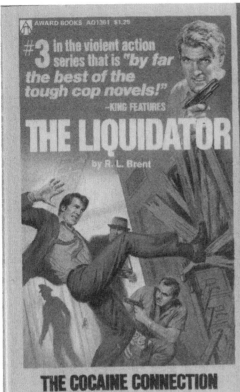

The cover reads:

AWARD BOOKS AO1361 $1.25

#3 In the violent action series that is "by far the best of the tough cop novels!"
—KING FEATURES

THE LIQUIDATOR
by R. L. Brent

THE COCAINE CONNECTION

I was able to find one on-line obituary which could have been the Larry Powell I was seeking. It listed a Larry J Powell Sr, who passed away at the age of 86 earlier this year. He was described as "a retired associate editor of the **Savannah Morning News** and **Savannah Evening Press** as well as the author of many books, magazine stories and articles," which fits the bill, as does the southern location of the newspapers in terms of tying in with Award. A veteran of the Korean War, Powell was survived by his wife of 65 years and two children.

When Award went under, Charter picked up some of their catalogue, specifically the Nick erarts the same group behind the hyperbolic sleaze-meets-tough-guy lines of Novel and Merit Books.

Powell also appeared in **Ellery Queen's Mystery Magazine** in 1969 with 'Double Exposure', and later in **True Action**, August 1974, with 'The Las Vegas Black Book Murders'. The latter title was from Magazine Management who owned Marvel Comics at this point. I am sure there are many, many more examples of Powell's writings in these types of publications, but I do not collect that stuff, and 99% of the information on men's pulps seems focused on the artists rather than the writers.

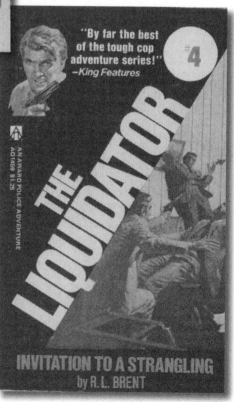

The cover reads:

"By far the best of the tough cop adventure series!"
—King Features

#4

AN AWARD POLICE ADVENTURE
AO1459 $1.25

THE LIQUIDATOR

INVITATION TO A STRANGLING
by R. L. BRENT

THE LIQUIDATOR

#**2** in a violent new action series

CONTRACT FOR A KILLING

by R. L. BRENT

"By far the best of the tough cop adventure series!" —*King Features*

copies of *Contract for a Killing* and *The Exchange*, so I am reliant on single copies offered by abebooks informing me of their existence. (I know of a collector who nearly want insane courtesy of abebooks when following the trail of a ludicrously priced single-copy of a western series he was researching. It did not exist as the listing was an error.)

One big cliché it may be, but The Liquidator is a glorious cliché and readers in search of a quick-hit in the tough cop genre could do far worst.

The Liquidator was evidently a popular name, also appearing on a Nick Carter book in 1973 (not written by Powell) and by John Gardner in 1965, a Boysie Oakes thriller which was filmed in 1968. Do not know how Award were able to publish a series if the name had been used on a film?

Carters. But they also reprinted the first four Liquidators and a new fifth, *The Exchange* (1978) which I am guessing they inherited it as a purchased but unpublished manuscript. I do not know if the Charters had small print runs and/or poor distribution, but I've only ever seen physical

DENNISON'S ARMY

Bantam evidently threw a chunk of change at the launch of the Dennison's War series, with the first instalment sporting a die-cut cover and double-page painting of the titular hit-squad. They must have been especially disappointed at having to shut the series down after only six titles, and based on the two books I've read, I share that disappointment.

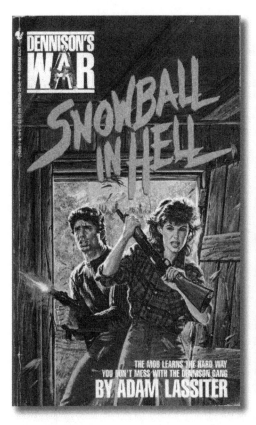

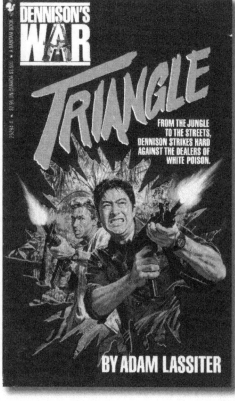

Men of Violence 5 and 6 reprint

Bantam evidently threw a chunk of change at the launch of the **Dennison's War** series, with the first instalment sporting a die-cut cover and double-page painting of the titular hit-squad. They must have been especially disappointed at having to shut the series down after only six titles, and based on the two books I've read, I share that disappointment.

The first book is split across two halves – the recruitment of the titular Army and their encounter with a renegade Vietnam colonel now acting as a crime kingpin. It does run out of steam before its 289 pages are played out, but it's as rough and a hard-boiled read as any I've encountered in the men's adventure genre. There is more than enough sleaze, degradation, blood and guts for even the most jaded of consumers. Take the opening scenes for example; a kidnap gone wrong at the hands of a psychopath; a bank-robbery in which one of the shot criminals has his head and hands hacked off by his colleagues to prevent identification; and a jail in a South American hell-hole which the Governor uses as his personal bordello. Subtle it ain't.

As so often is the case, the opening sequence detailing *The Magnificent Seven* style recruitment of the four hand-selected members of the Army is the most fun. Although I am always left wondering why they are

being held prisoner or are broke and destitute if they are they truly are the supposed killer elite. Dennison's pick includes Matt Conte a Mafia hit-man attempting to start his life over, Vang an ex-Guerilla leader and kung-fu master, an idealistic freedom fighter Chris Amado and a regular Army colonel. Dennison, and his alluring assistant Miss Paradise, are secretly employed by the government to deal with issues that threaten the American way of life without the normal politics and bureaucracy.

I imagine the thinking behind having a team, rather than a single character, was so that Bantam could revolve the lead each title, but Chris and Conte are the characters most often featured. Author Adam Lassiter characterisation of Chris is more well-rounded than the typical female character in the genre, and a damn sight more dangerous. Across the books she bloodi-

ly dispatches several goons – gut-shots a speciality - and has a fine line in *Commando*-style puns. There is also a blossoming romance between the two, but unfortunately Lassiter's dialogue is clunky and cliched; I cannot imagine he found much work in the romance paperbacks!

As typical of the genre, Lassiter was a pseudonym, in this case for Steven Krauzer who wrote a trio of Mack Bolans and contributed to the Cord western series before this assignment. Although his dialogue is not a strong-point, Krauzer's characterisation is excellent, with his descriptions of low-life's, violent red-necks, bereft gamblers and hench-men delivered in a hugely evocative and enjoyable style. Imagine the cantina scene from Star Wars rebooted for men's adventure fiction and you will get an idea of Krauzer's vision.

Krauzer is not shy about pouring on the sleaze, with several scenes involving sexual violence being especially distasteful, although unusually enough a man is on the receiving end of some of the treatment. Violence is for the most part applied sparingly but with real impact, and I was shocked by the scene in the bank in particular, with its callous logic to removing the head and hands. Overall, the first instalment in **Dennison's Army**

doesn't qualify as a must-read, but it delivers solid thrills for a mid-80's adventure pulp with the bonus of the darkly-humorous depictions of those populating the outskirts of the underworld.

As a **Men of Violence** bonus I also read the third entry, *Hell on Wheels*, as it featured outlaw bikers, a long-term favourite theme of mine. Chris Amado is chosen by Dennison to infiltrate a biker gang in an attempt to break their growing criminal influence. Evidently researched by watching several cable TV exposes on bik-

DENNISON SHOULD HAVE KILLED MITCHELL HORN WHEN HE HAD THE CHANCE A LONG TIME AGO —BUT HE DIDN'T. NOW, DENNISON'S OWN LIFE AND THE FUTURE OF THE COUNTRY ARE IN HORN'S HANDS!

Men of Violence 5 and 6 reprint

BEHIND THE BIKES, THE BEATINGS AND THE BEER ROARED AN UNSTOPPABLE CRIMINAL MACHINE— UNTIL DENNISON SENT IN CHRIS AMADO TO SHUT IT DOWN.

ers, this reminded me, in a good way, of the New English Library Hell's Angel's pulps of the early 1970's in the UK, in which the stories' hero would infiltrate the biker gang, providing the author ample opportunity to detail the piss-and-blood-stained initiation rituals and crusty culture. While simultaneously condemning it.

If Krauzer had approached *Hells on Wheels* with the unrestrained and at times tasteless approach of the first book in the series, we may have had some sort of sleaze classic on our hands. He doesn't, but we are still left with an up-tempo romp led by a strong female lead and populated by larger-than-life characters such as a gang of harpy bikers who castrate men with razors and a biker overlord called Ape Man with a bulk to match and teeth filed into points.

I've yet to be convinced as to the quality of men's adventure fiction of the 1980's, but the **Dennison's Army** series has been an eye-opener and has forced me to abandon my 1970's bias in search of other series worthy of documentation.

DENNISON'S WAR

A BANTAM BOOK ★ ★ $2.95 ★ ★ 24956-7

HELL ON WHEELS

THE FIREFIGHT FOR FREEDOM IS HEATING UP.
BY ADAM LASSITER

Men of Violence 5 and 6 reprint

BLOODY BRITS

**It's interesting to compare the wildly
differing approaches to cover illustrations
between the US and the UK for the same titles.
UK publishers such as New English Library,
Futura and Sphere would often carry covers far
more explicit in terms of nudity and violence than
their US counterparts, although
typically the contents were far tamer.**

Certainly, photo-covers were very much in vogue in the UK, and more
prevalent than illustrations in the late 60s and early 70s. Correspondent
Brian Emrich has labelled this phenomenon, "Bloody Brits".

Certainly the Sphere photo-covers for the Don Miles series aren't that
"Bloody", but I can't think of any other cover from the late 60s featuring a
trio of leather-clad female bikers in sunglasses and swastika armbands!

Men of Violence 5 and 6 reprint

Don Miles

CHALLENGE AT LE MANS

Larry Kenyon

Don meshes gears with a sex-mad Baroness in a plot to blow up half of Europe!

5/–

SPHERE

Men of Violence 5 and 6 reprint

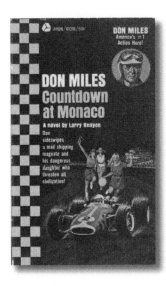  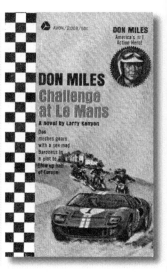

I'm sure there were specialist magazines sold under the counter in Soho or Times Square with less fetishistic covers. And a decade before punk adopted that look as a uniform. Photography is credited to Holmes Kitley Associates, a short-lived but influential London agency from the tail-end of the Swinging Sixties, who also provide the photo for *Countdown at Monaco*.

Compare to the paintings for the Avon US editions, which may have carried a clever graphic representation of a chequered flag down the spine, reflecting the racing theme, but featured small paintings by Don Stivers which were unusually flat and sterile. With lines like "fasten your seatbelts for excitement!" and "Don Miles America's #1 Action Hero!" they looked much more like children's books, or even tie-ins to a TV series or an action figure. Admittedly you didn't need to ask for a brown-paper bag to take them home in.

My favourite Don Miles cover is the photo, by Barrie Wenzell, for *The Devil's Ring* which showed a bikini-clad girl sporting a harpoon gun so phallic it would make Freud blush and made me think they should have issued 3-D glasses with the first printing.

What of the content of the books? There were four in the series, all released by Avon in the US in 1967 and reprinted in the UK by Sphere in 1968. Written by Lou Louderback as Larry Kenyon, surely one of the few examples of a pseudonym being more believable than the real name, they were produced for Lyle Kenyon Engel as part of his business producing series packages. Engel was something of a gear-head and wanted a series that combined racing cars with Nick Carter. On that basis he succeeded.

Miles is a millionaire through oil but dedicates his time to racing cars and perfecting his Texan drawl, until he is approached by

SPEED a secret agency that wants to recruit him. After fabricating a near-fatal crash they put him through intensive training and give him a set of weapons. All very Carter-esque, but with a lot of technical detail on cars and racing, that as a non gear-head was like reading a broken plate. Not that Louderback was space-filling, as he still weaves an intricate plot that increases in complexity and decreases in credibility throughout.

This was a real chore to wade through, comparable to lesser Carter of that period. The best scene is where Miles is downed by a knee to the balls from one of the biker vixens - I can't think of many men of violence captured in this way. There was nothing that made me want to read the other three, nor check out any of Louderback's contributions to the Carter series. Possibly of more interest were Louderbacks' non-fiction accounts of gangsters and

Don Miles

THE DEVIL'S RING

5/-

Don locks wheels with two treacherous dollies, and fights what may be the first battle of World War Three.

Larry Kenyon

SPHERE

molls for Fawcett, also from that period.

Overall, the Don Miles series is – *note to self, think up pithy one-liner with a car pun, like, never gets out of first gear, stalls at the starting line, their only value is as scrap, etc.*

SUBMISSION

The Dragonhead Deal by Richard J Harper may have been published in 1975, but reads as if it was written a decade earlier—and here I mean that as a positive.

It's missing the cynicism, testosterone overload and uber-violence typical of the genre in the 70's, but more than compensates for this as a tightly plotted, no-frills thriller with memorable characters and believable dialogue. This is the type of stream-lined and self-contained book that Gold Medal specialised in, and I think it would have been very much at home at that iconic publisher. I can imagine a desperate editor, faced with a gaping hole in their publishing schedule, rummaging through a pile of manuscripts that had been gathering dust and praising Odin when they stumbled across this surprise package.

I always avoid looking at the back cover of books ahead of reading them, as I do not like the copy-editor summarising for me in a paragraph the first half of a story and any of its twists. I am especially glad to have maintained that habit with *The Dragonhead Deal* and, if my opening paragraph has made you want to obtain the book, suggest you do not read on too much further for fear of the dreaded spoilers.

It got off to a mixed start, introducing Nathan Horn as the lead character, charming and sophisticated but with the morally-dubious job of arms dealer—presumably thus garnering little reader sympathy. However, it then throws in a thrilling opening set piece in which Horn is honey-trapped before, back at a low-rent motel, being subjected to an attempted drowning. Morgana Cross, a naïve small-town girl looking for adventure, saves Horn's life and is quickly drawn into his murky world of semi-legitimate deals and double-crossing.

It really starts motoring when Horn's nemesis Turtoro enters the scene, a corpulent and voracious sexual predator with an eye-patch, who harbours desires for Morgana and has designs on the arms shipment Horn is brokering. However, Turtoro and Horn both find themselves subject to manipulation and double-crosses by their respective paymasters, thus forcing then into an uneasy alliance.

Much of the action takes place in the unusual location of a submarine, of which author Harper makes excellent use, and sprinkles with believable details. The submarine is crewed by a veteran German U-boat commander and his salty sea dogs, who find their smuggling mission becoming infinitely more complex as Horn and Turtoro lock horns.

Across the book, the cynical and amoral Horn is transformed by the love of Morgana and is eventually able to repay her the favour of saving his life, but at quite some personal cost. Harper also shows that heroism and bravery are not restricted to a particular race or belief system, which was a refreshingly nuanced viewpoint.

Harper was an author I had not previously encountered and information about him is frustratingly scarce. I did find an on-line obituary which stated his life-span as 1928-2012, and listed Harper as having been a US marine, a forest ranger and a border patrol man, so he evidently walked the

walk. The on-line bibliographies do not list *The Dragonhead Deal*, but call out *Kill Factor* (1984) as a Edgar Award nominee, alongside two novels in a Tom Ragnon series about a Arizona patrolman. Earlier work is suggested as being for fiction magazines, specialising in westerns, but I could not see anything on Google to back this up.

I will be keeping an eye out for Harper's by-line in the future as I was absolutely knocked-out by this zinger. *The Dragonhead Deal* is the 200-page pulp equivalent of a torpedo: stream-lined, efficient, and delivering one hell of an explosive ending.

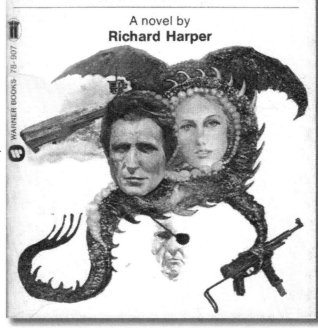

A top-secret arms shipment, a hijack no survivor would dare to report and an impossible love that happened anyway.

THE DRAGONHEAD DEAL

A novel by
Richard Harper

WARNER BOOKS 78-907

LOST IN TRANSLATION

In a country which has originated some truly unique paperback 'men of violence'—think TNT and Malko—one of the most famous and successful French series was San-Antonio. France loved its hard-boiled detectives, inventing the label 'film noir', and was the first to celebrate American crime authors Jim Thompson and David Goodis.

In contrast, super-intendant San Antonio was flippant, free-wheeling and littered his first-person narration with slang and complex-puns. Pretty much the opposite of the dark and gritty world of the celebrated 'noir'. Against the odds, much like the anti-heroes in the men's adventure fiction genre, San Antonio prevailed, going on to about 175 paperback adventures and selling millions of books in the process.

San Antonio's creation, by Frederic Dard (1921-2000), was commercially motivated having experienced poverty first-hand, with teenage memories fresh of his parents' belongings seized by debt collectors. These financial difficulties resulted in the family moving to Lyon where he worked in his Uncle's garage, who recognised Dard's talent as a writer, helping him secure a journalistic job at the local paper. It's here that the young Dard first encountered the seamier side of life when he became the title's crime reporter.

By 1940 Dard had his first novel published and was inspired to pursue a career in the theatre. This was a failure and with a real need for quick cash, he decided to knock out a commercially angled book, drawing on his experience as a journalist and using thriller-author Peter Cheyney as his template.

British-born Cheyney was one of those writers massive in his time, but all but forgotten now – in the 1950's his Lemmy Caution detective thrillers written in a quasi-American style (a common approach, my dad once swore blind to me that Hank Janson was American, and was more than a little disappointed when I told him the truth) which sold millions world-wide and were adapted into films in France.

KNIGHTS OF
ARABIA

San
Antonio

SPHERE

Men of Violence 5 and 6 reprint

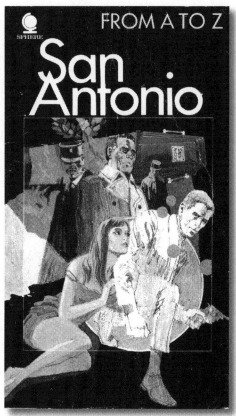

The name of the San Antonio character and author (the stories are in the first person) were chosen by Dard randomly pointing his finger at a American map. Paris-based super-intendant San splits his time between working for his wise but decrepit Inspector and the enigmatic "Old Man", who sets him secret service style missions. San is often accompanied by his slobbish right-hand man Berurier whose lack of breeding and massive frame proves both a help and a hindrance.

With San Antonio, Dard rivaled Cheyney's commercial success, purportedly selling 27 million copies in France, a phenomenal amount in a country with a population of 60 million. Surprisingly

for a best-seller, he was also embraced by the critics due to the strong core of satire running through the books, and his seemingly unlimited capacity for wordplay, puns and euphemisms for the sexual act. Apparently at one point there was even a San-Antonio Dictionary produced.

There are ten English-language translations of the San Antonio books for us to sample. In the UK there were six editions which appeared from Sphere Books in 1969, with all being reprinted by Paperback Library in the US in 1970. Plus an extra two, which never appeared in UK paperback. To even things up, there were two

UK hardback editions which were never printed in the US. All the paperbacks use the same cover art, although in such a different way it's not immediately noticeable.

There were two translators responsible for the English-language versions, with Cyril Buhler chalking up nearly twice as many as Hugh Campbell. If both of the original books were written in the same vein, Campbell's version of *From A to Z* reads significantly differently to Buhler's translation of *Knights of Arabia*.

In *A to Z*, the story- of San Antonio pretending he has been assassinated to draw the perpetrators out of hiding- is lost beneath the lay-

TOUGH JUSTICE

San Antonio

ers of word-play and foot-notes. The latter explain some of the more obscure or complex puns and information, such as *"A rude French pun – for specialists only"* or *"If you did not get that one, you've no right to be reading my books"*.

My personal tolerance for such tomfoolery is low, even less so when there is such a large volume and they are so obscure. This large proportion of wisecracks and laconic asides from San Antonio compared to the actual thriller elements of the story, meant *A to Z* was purely farce with no sense of tension or excitement.

Translated by Buhler, *Knights of Arabia* sends San Antonio to the Middle East to investigate a pair of missing agents, and is more successful in terms of delivering an adventure novel, with a greater balance between plot and Dard's word-play. Comparing the size of the type between the two books, I would estimate that Buhler's word count was 25% higher than Campbell's *A to Z*, which assuming the source material was of a similar length, suggests to me that Campbell vision of Dard's word was far more stream-lined. Unfor-

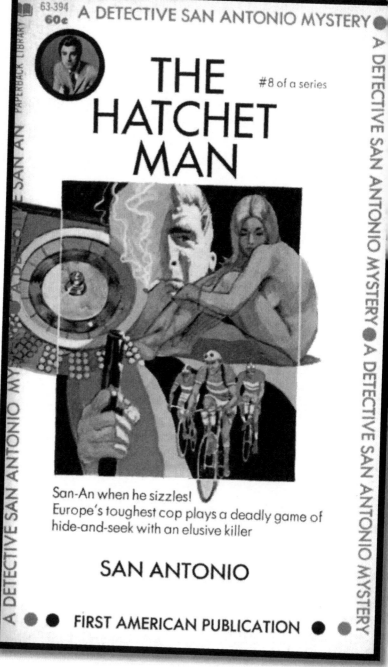

63-394
60¢

A DETECTIVE SAN ANTONIO MYSTERY ●

SAN AN PAPERBACK LIBRARY

A DETECTIVE SAN ANTONIO MYSTERY ● A DETECTIVE SAN ANTONIO MYSTERY ● A DETECTIVE SAN ANTONIO MYSTERY

THE HATCHET MAN

#8 of a series

San-An when he sizzles!
Europe's toughest cop plays a deadly game of hide-and-seek with an elusive killer

SAN ANTONIO

A DETECTIVE SAN ANTONIO MYSTERY

● ● ● FIRST AMERICAN PUBLICATION ● ● ●

tunately it was the exciting pieces that he removed.

While reflecting on my experience with these two San Antonio's, I am reminded of the anecdote about Peter Benchley's *Jaws* being about infidelity rather than a giant shark. I do not think I quite understand what the San Antonio books are really about, due to cultural differences and the passing of half-a-century since they were written, but they are definitely not about a spy committing acts of derring-do. I can admire Dard's ballet of word-play and respect the translators tasked with keeping its spirit and wit intact for the English language, but cannot recommend tracking the books down.

They are rare on the used-book market. I do not know whether this is because the books are collectible, or the print runs were low and copies just have not survived the intervening years. Of the Sphere versions, I have only personally encountered two while book-shopping over the decades, of which only one is currently available for sale online. US versions are available, but not in large numbers.

Despite his commercial success, Dard's personal life was not always a happy one. Apparently he tried to escape his unhappy first marriage by hanging himself (methinks serving divorce papers would have been as effective), and a daughter from his second wife was kidnapped for ransom. When he died of a heart attack in 2000, the French president spoke of the matter, which surely must be a first for any writer in the pulp school.

THE GREAT GAME

RENEGADE is one of those western series that I push to men's adventure readers that tell me they do not like westerns (the other being Fargo). Although packaged by Warner as westerns, they are actually about a soldier-of-fortune plying his trade in Central and South America, set in the *Wild Bunch* era of the late 1800's when the cowboy was a dying breed.

The titular Renegade (although, interestingly, he is never called this in the books, being more commonly referred to as Captain Gringo) is Captain Richard Walker, a court-martialled cavalry officer who escapes a hangman's noose to lead a life as a free-wheeling soldier-of-fortune in the politically volatile landscape of Central to South America. Gaston is his side-kick, an ex-Legionnaire whose cynical and at times brutal world-view keeps Gringo out of trouble–to an extent.

Renegade author 'Ramsay Thorne' was actually Lou Cameron, prolific as a writer and illustrator for comics in the 1950's before turning his hand to paperbacks in the 60's and 70s. I covered off some of his war and tough cop pot-boilers in a previous issue, noting his skill in recreating the confusion of battle in his works. Besides sharing this trait (which provides my favourite scene in a **Renegade**, if you read on) Cameron's **Renegades** are characterised by the rich socio-political detail he brings to their exotic settings, the labyrinthine plot strands which he somehow pulls together at the end, authentic portrayal of military tactics, cynical humour, brutal violence and kinky sex. What's not to like?

Unsurprisingly when produced in such short order, some books are superior to others, and you will read my thoughts as to which and why in a few capsule reviews below. I would not recommend 'bingeing' on the **Renegades**, as when you read several of these books in quick succession, as I did for this article, Cameron's formula soon becomes apparent; starting point is Gringo forced into accepting a dirty mission of subterfuge by a politician or agent of an amoral government; two female foils, one a sympathetic love-interest and the other a sexually super-charged double-agent; Gringo and Gaston separated but reunited by the story's end; plenty of back-stabbing, and no real winners.

Renegade
Book 1, 1979

Unlike many men's adventure characters, Gringo has an entire novel dedicated to his back-story and it's told in linear style rather than as a flash-back. Much of the action takes place in Mexico with Gringo meeting Gaston in a hell-hole jail, before making an ingenious escape from the firing squad (this is where Gringo picks up the huge machine-gun that later becomes his trade-mark weapon). Joining up with a group of Mexican revolutionaries they hijack a stream train and go on a hectic journey with what seems like the entire government forces in pursuit.

There are some great cat and mouse scenes between the train-bound Gringo and a wily officer on the opposition as they attempt to outwit each oth-er. Not all the ingredients I listed in the introduction were in place in this first instalment, so Cameron was evidently still developing his formula, but it's a rollicking adventure novel all the same.

He's unshakable, unstoppable, unkillable...Captain Gringo, the Legend of the Border!

Renegade 1

An Adult Western

RamsayThorne

88 992 WARNER BOOKS

Death Hunter

Book 4, 1980

By the fourth volume Cameron has already honed his approach, and this a stellar example of the type of labyrinth plotting and double-crossing that differentiated the Renegade books from other series. Gringo is caught between the manipulative British spy Greystoke, who will become a recurring character, and the Germans, whom Greystoke believes are building a submarine base in Costa Rica which will give them control of the Panama Canal.

The plot's complexities only become explained in the final chapter, so this is undoubtedly a book that does require your concentration, and if you are guilty of being a "skimmer" (guilty as charged) you may well find yourself scratching your head and re-reading the closing sections. There is plenty of earthy sex and humour, often combined, with Gringo over-powered by the frustrated and big-boned fraulein who lives with a German plantation owner, and a mother and daughter who alternately show their gratitude to a saddlesore Gringo while unaware of the other's actions and individually swearing him to secrecy.

There is a great vignette where Gringo is drilling the rag-tag team of mercenaries and drunks he has quickly assembled to sail down the Canal with. When one shows insubordination, Gaston jumps on his head and kills him to instil discipline in the make-shift crew. It's later revealed that the dead man is nothing of the sort, and it was a set-up pre-arranged to send a message to a potentially rebellious group.

Hell Raider
Book 9. 1981

A more tongue-in-cheek approach to this adventure as Gringo and Gaston are hired by a beautiful archaeologist to steer a steam boat up the Amazon in search of her missing father who had been investigating lost civilisations. Certainly the scene in which Gringo encounters a tribe of Amazonians who grease themselves up and wrestle him and his partner is OTT even by the standard of this series. A smaller cast of characters and with much of the action taking place on the boat, I found this to be a lesser account of Renegade's exploits.

Captain Gringo— no man can stop him, no woman wants to.

WARNER BOOKS 90-550 $1.95

Renegade

HELL RAIDER

9

An Adult Western

Ramsay Thorne

The Great Game
Book 10, 1981

Caught between the US and the Britain in an undeclared war, Gringo and Gaston find themselves escorting two vulnerable nuns across a de-stabilised Venezuela. Of course, the nuns are anything but that, and their sweaty sex scenes dominate many pages.

An apt title, referring to the actions of governments and their spy-masters who often see their manipulation of people's lives as if they were pawns in a game. I found the plotting and pace a bit too languid, and it lost me before the end. But I have to caveat that with this being the fifth of the series I read in short succession.

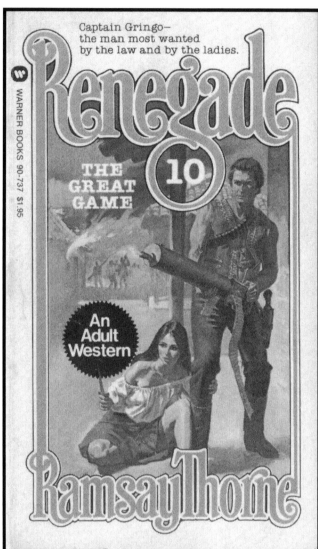

Captain Gringo—
the man most wanted
by the law and by the ladies.

WARNER BOOKS 90-737 $1.95

Renegade

10

THE GREAT GAME

An Adult Western

Ramsay Thorne

It does contain my favourite Renegade vignette – the books open with the boat carrying Gringo and Gaston toward a jetty, above which is a group of battle-tough mercenaries ready to ambush and slaughter the pair with their machine-guns. When the bullet-ridden bodies of the mercenaries are found with no trace of Gringo, his legend as an indestructible warrior only increases. Cameron then reveals that the pair were oblivious as they had sniffed a rat and leapt overboard before the docking, and the mercenaries killed each other after a petty argument escalated.

THE EXECUTIONER VERSUS MICHIGAN GENERAL CORP

MEN OF VIOLENCE contributor Andreas Decker tipped me off to the on-line presence of detailed reports on several court cases involving Don Pendleton's THE EXECUTIONER series. Designed for use by law students, all were full of technical jargon and detail, but all the same were fascinating accounts of the cut and thrust of the fast-fiction industry and threw up some interesting points around creativity and ownership.

I have attempted to distil material which ran to thirty-odd A4 pages down into just eight A5 pages; also, I have no legal qualifications ('Really?' I hear you cry!), so please bear in mind that my interpretation of the material may well be off. Material in italics has been directly lifted from the reports.

The earliest court case I located was from August 1979, an action for 'breach of contract' taken by Michigan General Corporation against a group of six plaintiffs who were the founders of Bee Line Books and later, Pinnacle Books. Of the six listed, the ones typically quoted in the case papers were David Zentner and Walter Weidenbaum, who were active in the company rather than the other four who were silent partners.

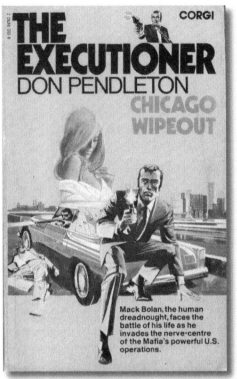

Michigan General had purchased Pinnacle Books for $2.7m in January 1973. They were an investment group that had no interest or expertise in publishing but specialised in acquiring small companies that had been successful and leaving them alone to continue making a profit. Crucial to Michigan's purchase of Pinnacle was the understanding that the publisher, rather than Don Pendleton, owned the rights to the huge-selling Executioner series. When this issue blew-up in the same year, Pendleton downed tools and signed contracts with New American Library. Michigan put forward in the court case that they had missed valuable sales during this period and have overpaid for Pinnacle.

The court papers list testimony from Don Pendleton, Dave Zentner (Managing Director of Bee-Line and Pinnacle), Walter Weidenbaum (Pinnacle's attorney), Andy Ettinger (Chief Editor at Pinnacle) and Stanley Springer (representing Michigan General). It includes details of how The Executioner was created, or certainly two versions of how The Executioner was created. Zentner does not come out of the testimony as the most credible or trustworthy of individuals, with one claim of his that was crucial to the case dismissed as by the judge as his invention. It is seemingly accepted by all sides that Pendleton was an unpredictable and hot-headed individual. I have no knowledge to challenge or back this up.

In 1965, David Zentner was the publisher of a series of men's magazines, such as **Topper**, which were distributed by the Kable News Company. You will often see their distinctive 'K' logo on paperback and magazine pubs of that era. With the sales of sleaze paperbacks increasing, Zentner approached Kable with a proposal; set up and distribute their own line of sleaze paperbacks with him at the helm. In the summer of 1965, he closed a deal with five men, including Walter Weidenbaum, who were then stockholders, officers, or employees of Kable.

Zentner was the president and chief operating officer of Bee-Line. The other plaintiffs were, for the most part, "silent partners" in the business, and Weidenbaum, an attorney, functioned as the liaison between Zentner and the other stockholders. Among the authors writing for Bee-Line was Donald Pendleton, who had been writing for sleaze paperbacks, including a series featuring Sewart Mann a tough P.I.

By 1968, Bee-Line had successfully experimented with some forays into general fiction, so decided to enter the "mass market" paperback industry. In May and June, they had several meetings with Lyle Engel, the famous packager of serial books such as Nick Carter which had been running at Award Books since 1964. Apparently Zentner and Weidenbaum were not particularly inspired by any of Engel's suggestions for a series, and they believed that they could develop a better concept themselves. In retrospect, I speculate that their experience with sleaze paperbacks, which often delved into the spy genre, suggested there was an audience for a tougher more abrasive style of serial fiction compared to the rather safe Nick Carter. Based on the court notes, here is their account of Bolan's creation-

According to Zentner and Weidenbaum, they were walking on Third Avenue in mid-town Manhattan, after a luncheon meeting with Engel, when the following conversation took place: Mr. Weidenbaum said to me [Zentner], "What do you think of an idea that just occurred to me? Suppose we use a man, an anti-hero type, who is a trained jungle fighter in Vietnam, and whose life is destroyed because his family has been damaged irrevocably by the Mafia, and who gets a leave of absence due to hardship from the Army, . . . comes home, finds these terrible conditions, and tries to go on an one-man crusade to eliminate this evil from the face of the earth?" And spontaneously he said, "Let's call him `The Executioner'."

I thought it was a tremendous title, tremendous name, for such an individual, and in further discussion Mr. Weidenbaum said to me, "Why not have him then, this Executioner, go from city to city, find the strongholds of the Mafia in each city, and destroy them in this single one-man campaign to eliminate the Mafia?"

In further discussion, Weidenbaum and Zentner named their character "Matt Bolan," and decided to approach Don Pendleton to see if he would be willing to write the books.

During a telephone conversation in mid-July 1968, Zentner outlined the Executioner concept to Pendleton. On or about August 19, 1968, Pendleton submitted a synopsis of the proposed book to Zentner, and in October, Pendleton signed a contract to write the book. The Executioner books, along with other mass market paperbacks, were published under the "Pinnacle" imprint or trade name, to avoid the taint of Bee-Line's reputation.

Pendleton's version of the inception of the series differs. Pendleton testified, at his deposition that, during the July telephone conversation, Zentner said that he was interested in manuscripts suitable for mass market publication. Pendleton acknowledged that Zentner had suggested the name "The Executioner" as an anti-hero protagonist at war with the underworld. Pendleton testified, however, that he told Zentner during the telephone conversation that he had "been developing a theme for over a year regarding a Viet Nam trained soldier who returns to this country and declares a holy war on organized crime." This was a result of a series of conversations that Pendleton had with third parties over a year before his conversation with Zentner. Additionally, Pendleton drew on his own military experience in developing this idea. Pendleton also claimed to have developed the name "Mack Bolan."

As most of us undoubtedly know, Mack Bolan was a huge success and by the beginning of 1972, the nine titles published date had sold more than four million copies. Zentner believed the market would take more Bolan books, so invited Pendleton to New York for three days so they could meet face to face for the first time. Shortly before Pendleton was due to leave to fly home, Zentner received negative answers when he asked whether the author could increase his productivity or consider using ghost-writers.

Zentner then stated that his suggestion was not entirely up to Pendleton because the series belonged to the publisher which could assign authors to write the books as it saw fit. This infuriated Pendleton, who proclaimed "Nobody else is going to write my books." After further heated discussion along these lines, Pendleton stormed out of the Bee-Line offices, into a waiting taxicab.

Upon Pendleton's return home, he wrote a letter to Zentner, dated January 21, 1972, reading in part: "Regarding our point of disagreement, just one postscript please. I will take whatever steps are necessary to insure a steady flow of Executioner books, of the quality and quantity desired, but this is and must be my personal responsibility. . . .

I am not a Pinnacle hired hand.

I do not rent myself (or my name) to anyone.

I do not write "on assignment." Let's keep those ideas visible in our association. Otherwise, I will be compelled to assert my legal position and I doubt that either of us wish to begin hurling legalities at each other. . . ."

Mack Bolan is my creation. All of the characters, incidents, plots, situations, and every word of dialogue used in each of the books are my creations. In a strictly legal sense, even "the Executioner" is my creation but I stand more on ethics than on legalities, and I would not contest your independent use of the Executioner tag. I would, however, descend with all the fury of an outraged plagiarism victim if any attempt was made to steal Mack Bolan and/or any of

his attendant creations. It is important that you understand that implicitly.

On receipt of this letter, Zentner convened a meeting of his staff, sending them a memorandum dated January 24, 1972, reading in part:

I think, at this stage, that if anything were done about another author he [Pendleton] might panic and either break down completely or force some unreasonable action in view of his basic emotional insecurities.

He made it unmistakable to me that he thinks he "owns" the series. Somehow, he believes that he even originated if not the idea itself just about everything else.

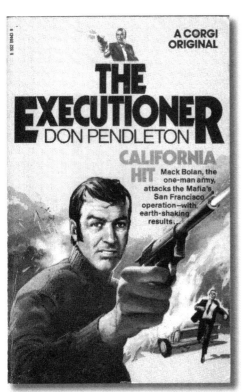 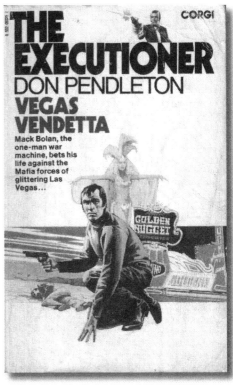

Men of Violence 5 and 6 reprint

Zentner, Ettinger (who was Pendleton's editor) and Weidenbaum met shortly afterwards to discuss the Pendleton situation. After Zentner and Weidenbaum recounted their version of the creation of the series, Weidenbaum suggested that a letter be sent to Pendleton. He prepared a handwritten draft of a letter for Zentner's signature that set out the development of the series and the position that the publisher was taking, namely, that the publisher created and owned the series and that while Bee-Line would be most pleased to have Pendleton continue to write, it would make other arrangements if necessary. After further discussion, it was decided that the letter might provoke Pendleton and could delay the receipt and publication of future books. Accordingly, it was decided that Zentner would telephone Pendleton in an attempt to bring him back into the fold. As to what next occurred, there are conflicting versions.

Zentner testified that shortly after the staff meeting he telephoned

CORGI

THE EXECUTIONER
DON PENDLETON

JERSEY GUNS

Death stalked Bolan along moonlit roads the night he returned to New Jersey–where a thousand Mafia guns were waiting for him...

0 552 08861 3

Pendleton, reminded him of the history of their relationship, and of how Pendleton's success was largely owing to Zentner's efforts. As a result of Zentner's comments, Pendleton became very contrite, apologized profusely for creating the incident, acknowledged the publisher's ownership of the series, and said that he was just upset about the idea of other authors. He told Zentner to tear up the original of the letter of January 21, and said that he withdrew the statements it contained, and was tearing up his own copy. Zentner then asked Pendleton to send a telegram withdrawing the letter, which Pendleton subsequently did.

Pendleton testified, at his deposition, that he never spoke to Zentner, or to anyone from Bee-Line, concerning the contents of his January 21 letter. He specifically denied telling Zentner to tear up the letter and stated that he did not send a telegram to Zentner.

Weidenbaum testified that Zentner told him, shortly after the meeting, that he had spoken with Pendleton and that Pendleton acknowledged that the publisher owned the series and had withdrawn his comments of January 21. Although Weidenbaum had requested that Zentner get something in writing from Pendleton which acknowledged the publisher's ownership of the series, he never saw the telegram from Pendleton, or any other writing to that effect.

Ettinger testified that he had no conversation with either Pendleton or Zentner regarding Zentner's alleged telephone call to Pendleton. Ettinger did not recall whether Zentner told him about Pendleton's instructions to tear up the letter. Nor, did Ettinger ever see the telegram. Nonetheless, Ettinger believed there had been a discussion between Pendleton and Zentner because "certain operating decisions were made shortly thereafter which seemed to calm the stormy waters." The existence of this telegram was questioned by the court, which dismissed it as a creation by Zentner would should be dismissed as evidence.

Specifically, "we began paying Mr. Pendleton more money and on a regular basis and one of the sources of his problem was that he was always in financially dire straits and the fact that we were paying him more money seemed to solve the problem, and I had assumed, although I was not told, we settled the problems."

CORGI

THE EXECUTIONER
DON PENDLETON
PANIC IN PHILLY

When Mack Bolan knew the Mafia guns were mobbing up in Philly, he reckoned it was time to hit town...

At about this time, Bee-Line was negotiating the sale of the motion picture rights to the Executioner to Avco Embassy Pictures. Pendleton learned of these negotiations, and in a letter to Zentner dated March 13, 1972, he revoked a power of attorney he had granted to Zentner to negotiate and execute such contracts on his behalf. Zentner telephoned Pendleton on March 17 and told him that the motion picture contract could make them both rich men, and that Pendleton's conduct was jeopardizing the deal. Pendleton evidently agreed, and in separate letters to Zentner, both dated March 20, Pendleton reinstated Zentner's power of attorney, and covered a signed copy of

THE EXECUTIONER

DON PENDLETON

CORGI

ASSAULT ON SOHO

Mack Bolan, America's one-man army rocks London in his war on the Mafia.

Pinnacle only and did not include the Bee-Line division)

As part of the due diligence that typically takes place in this type of deal, Sidney Springer acted for Michigan General. Springer was to uncover some issues which would eventually come back to bite them. When a deal was signed in mid-72 (but not completed until January 1973), Zentner warranted *"that no single author and no single series, such as the Executioner series, accounts for more than 30% of the sales volume of the Company or of the Pinnacle Line."* In lay-man's terms, Springer wanted to ensure they weren't putting "all their eggs in one basket", namely a Donald Pendleton one.

It was later revealed that actually 50% of the eggs were in the Pendleton basket! One of defendant's officers did testify that the Executioner series accounted for about 50% of the company's profit in 1972, which in basic maths mean Michigan General paid about $1.25 million for the rights to a series they might not even own!

Also Springer discovered that Bee-Line/Pinnacle were not always correctly registering copyright in the name of the publisher rather than the author. He sought opinion from a New York law firm well-versed in the legalities of publishing and they

the motion picture contract with a letter to Zentner, reading in part:

"My wife told me, David, nearly four years ago, that David Zentner was going to make me rich one day. . . . . From the bottom of my heart, Dave, thank you.

In mid-1972, Bee-Line changed its corporate name to Carlyle Communications, Inc. which continued to use the Bee-Line name as an imprint or trade name for its erotic paperbacks, and the name "Pinnacle" for its mass market paperbacks. (when Michigan General completed the purchase, it was backed up his initial view in a letter stating -

After reviewing the various contracts and letters that exist by and between Pinnacle [Carlyle] and Don Pendleton, the author of The Executioner series, it is our opinion that, except for the limited rights specified in the papers, Pinnacle does not have any right or claim of right with respect to the character Mack Bolan, the central figure in the series, as against Pendleton's subsequent use thereof.

. . . . .

As between Pinnacle and Pendleton, the whole question of scope of copyright protection is slightly irrelevant because Pinnacle has simply failed to tie up all of the rights in and to the series as well as the character portrayed.

. . . Thus, if Michigan General is set on acquiring character and series rights of substance, it is essential that Pendleton and Pinnacle enter into a new contract drafted properly to provide for same.

Springer relayed to Michigan that they were running the risk that Zentner had over-played his role in the creation of The Executioner, so they should seek a legally binding warranty from Zentner, and also approach Pendleton to confirm Pinnacle owned the copyright.

But in the case of the latter, they should consider making an approach after the take-over for fear of upsetting Pendleton.

Springer received two letters from Pinnacle in response. The first, from Weidenbaum stated:

Dave [Zentner] assured me that he met with Pendleton, gave him our ideas for plot, locale, and principal characters and that it was clearly understood between them that the series title "Executioner" series, the war with the Mafia concept, and characters, particularly Mack

Bolan, would belong to our corporation.

The second letter in December 1972, was from Zentner:

[W]e have always approved, and still do before any book is written or contracted for the basic plot, the locale and a general outline of the story. Don Pendleton has publicly and in many conversations with both myself, my editor and other staff members, always willingly and gratefully acknowledged the fact that we created the EXECU-TIONER idea and concept, and that he started working originally on an assignment basis.

Springer was discouraged by Zentner from approaching Pendle-ton directly, stating that contract discussions would distract Pendleton from producing his highly-profitable books. Michigan General presumably decided that the risks were manageable or would not ever come to fruition and the purchase of Pinnacle went ahead in January 1973.

Pendleton however was about to throw the cat amongst the pigeons that same month. While visiting the Pinnacle offices to discuss finances, as he had made more money in 1972 than any other year, he sensed an "atmosphere" which made him feel "uneasy".

When he received the contract for book 16 in the series, which was the same as the previous contract, for some reason Pendleton decided to take it to a literary agent who in the future would liaise with Pinnacle on his behalf. Michigan General had actually requested that Pendleton's contract be changed as part of their take-over, but editor Ettinger replicated the existing contract and issued it without Zentner seeing it. Pure speculation on my part, but I wonder if Ettinger tipped off Pendleton as to the Michigan deal and its potential implications.

Pendleton's agent then began to shop the Bolan series around to other publishers for a better financial deal. In February 1973, Pendleton wrote to Ettinger and told him to remove the 16th book, *Sicilian Slaughter*, from the publishing schedule. That same month, Pendleton signed a contract with New American Library for the series. Pinnacle responded in two ways – they farmed the 16th book out to William Crawford, who wrote it as Jim Petersen and launched The Penetrator series.

Pendleton took legal action against *Sicilian Slaughter* and despite being printed in May, distribution was delayed

until the end of July. Pinnacle also successfully applied for a block on New American Library publishing or promoting Mack Bolan.

In November 1973, while the appeal was sub judice, Pendleton and Pinnacle settled their dispute. The settlement agreement is dated November 12, 1973, and it provides, among other things, that Pendleton would terminate his contract with The New American

CORGI

THE EXECUTIONER
JIM PETERSON

SICILIAN SLAUGHTER

Mack Bolan hits the Mafia's birthplace
–and Sicily starts to sizzle...

Library and return to Pinnacle; that Pendleton would write six more Executioner books for Pinnacle; that Pinnacle had an option, which it could exercise in six-book blocks, to publish further Executioner books by Pendleton; that Pinnacle could release Sicilian Slaughter; that Pendleton would be required to produce four books each year; that Pendleton would receive a royalty of 12.5% of the retail price on net sales of the books; that Pendleton owned the copyright to all future books; and, that he had been the owner of the copyright to the Executioner books previously published.

THE EXECUTIONER
DON PENDLETON
CARIBBEAN KILL
CORGI

Mack Bolan, the one-man army, tracks the Mafia to their sunny island hideaways – and the lush vacation isles were never hotter

Due to the delays caused by this case, Pinnacle was able to publish only two Executioner books in 1973. Based on a typical rate of five volumes a year, Michigan General later sued Zentner and co for lost profits on the three books, in the region of $274k. Zentner's response was that Michigan had purchased a lucrative business and pointed to their growth in volumes in 1973 compared to previous years. Specifically from 2.7m volumes in 1971 to 5m in 1972 to 8.6m books in 1973. Gross sales went from $1.5m in 1971 to $2.5m in 1972 to $4.6m in 1973.

The case was appealed in April 1980 and decided in October 1980.

More to come next issue.

Printed in Poland
by Amazon Fulfillment
Poland Sp. z o.o., Wrocław